T0064503

ATTITUDE OF GRATITUDE

EBONY SIMMS

authorHOUSE®

AuthorHouse™
1663 Liberty Drive
Bloomington, IN 47403
www.authorhouse.com
Phone: 1 (800) 839-8640

Published by AuthorHouse   08/11/2015

ISBN: 978-1-5049-2848-9 (sc)
ISBN: 978-1-5049-2847-2 (e)

Contents

Over the years I've received a lot of questions about my writings. Mostly questions asking if this is truth or fiction. My response is always that art imitates life and life imitates art and I leave it at that. Unlike the books I've written before this is my truth.

I have come a long way and would like to tell you that Gratitude has changed my life in some very amazing ways. Once I began to refocus my energies and truly believe that there is a greater force in the Universe, people, places and events began to take form in my life.

As I write I pray that no one will be offended by my word selection. I believe that everyone has a vehicle in which they express their art and this just happens to be mine. In this book I refer to God but whatever you feel comfortable calling the higher power call it what you will.

Please do not take the short length of this book as not being serious content. I have just taken out any fluff and have made this as simple and as easy to understand as possible.

Ebony Simms

To my God I am grateful that you accept me as I am. To Jesus I am grateful that you came into my life. To the Holy Spirit thank you so much for leading and guiding me every day of my life. To my guardian angel Shirley "Pooh Bear" Mitchell I am grateful that you instilled love in me.

~ Introduction ~

Before I got to this point of where I am today, yet still moving forward I was extremely depressed. My grandmother that raised me Shirley "Pooh Bear" Mitchell had recently died and I didn't make it to her funeral because of an argument with my oldest daughter's father. I had been feeling real sorry for myself. I was sixty pounds over weight and eating myself further and further into massive depression. All of my bills were upside down and the more I worked, it seemed the further in debt I was getting. At one point I wanted to just give up and die.

The relationships around me were at an all time low and I was at my wits end with the relationship of my youngest daughter's father. I would wake up sad and go to bed crying. I was having a horrible time at my job and I kept asking myself how could I get out of this mess? I sat in this white chair in my room and tried to relax as I flipped the remote I came across a series of infomercials and one was with Anthony Robbins.

After watching the infomercial on Anthony Robbins and his life changing series I went online and looked up some sites on self motivation and daily affirmations. Robbins says "you must have unreasonable thinking and this will defy the odds and these are the most successful people."

The first step is changing the way your mind thinks. You want to start having positive thinking and positive self-talk. But far beyond positive thinking you have to know that there is a source greater than you and I. If friends and family are not supportive or they are negative you have to separate yourself from them. Sometimes it's not easy to separate from them so you must encourage yourself that much more. You must tell yourself that you can do whatever you set your mind to. Such as if you want to be a business owner start thinking that you are a business owner now. You will succeed and your business will grow. You are a child of God and He loves you and He is happy that you did not give up and die.

I took these messages and began my research of Self-Help meaning these are the things that helped me and I am passing them on and just maybe they will help you. I am not a medical doctor or a professional on the subject matter but I do know what has helped and continues to help me.

Attitude of Gratitude

Chapter 1

~ Gratitude ~

Gratitude is not only the greatest of the virtues but the parent of all others. Cicero (106 BC-43 BC)

𝔍 pulled out my 𝔄ttitude of 𝔊ratitude journal and began to flip through the pages…on my first entry 𝔍 wrote;

While sitting out by the lake I find refuge in God's grace and mercy. I find gratitude in knowing that He walks with me and never forsakes me. I love and honor His name and take comfort in knowing there is a source that I can tap into. As long as I stay connected to Him I feel encouraged.

It's when I turn away from the source that I feel my deepest despair. Today in this very moment which is the only moment I can ever be in I have an attitude of gratitude. I am in love with life and all things of it. I am in love with the peace of mind that I have. Today my peace is inside of me. Life is ever changing and whatever does not change dies. I have the grace of change today. I will find gratitude in all things, and it will be life altering.

As I think back to some of my early childhood memories I am reminded of my grandmother coming to pick me up on Sunday mornings to take me with her to church. It was out of the way of her route but still she would make it a point to come to get me. The name of the church is New Life Mission for All Souls with Pastor Rosa Lenzy. Although this is not the first church I remember attending this is the first church that I was involved in and really heard the word of God.

My mother and I lived in a one bedroom apartment on the fourth floor of what was called Kings Square in Landover, Maryland. I remember my father being there for a short time then leaving; then my brother moved in for a while but left as well. I remember spending a lot of time in that apartment alone from about the ages of five until maybe eleven. During those long days alone while my mother worked double shifts or attended nightly card games, I always felt that there was a presence there watching me. I would think to myself that there was a little camera installed in the corner of the living room ceiling and if anything went wrong whoever was watching would come in and save me. I have now come to learn that the presence was the Holy Spirit.

When my grandmother would bring me home from our day of church she would fold up a $20 bill really tight and put it in my hand. Then she would tell me don't let your mother know you have this money. I want you to take it and buy yourself some groceries for the week. I quickly learned to look forward to going to church with my grandmother on Sunday morning because I could guarantee that I would be able to eat for the week. This taught me a valuable lesson in gratitude. I was so grateful that my grandmother cared enough about me to make sure that I would eat for the week as she gave the money to me with so much love and compassion.

As years passed my mother could no longer afford to keep us in the apartment so she sent me to live with my grandmother. At the time I didn't understand and I felt a great loss because I had never lived without my mother before. Even though she was not home during the day she would always come home at night and make sure I was tucked into bed and I would surely miss that.

Moving in with my grandmother I had everything I could have needed and there was always someone home with me. It was four of us that shared a room, my grandmother, my aunt, my cousin and I. Being there I was never alone but I could say that I was lonely. There were often times my mother would call me and I would cry that I missed her and when was she coming back to get me. I didn't want to be a burden to my grandmother so I would clean the entire house and tried my best to stay out of everyone's way. I spent a lot of time just sitting on my bed thinking and reflecting on my life. I had the top bunk so I would stay up there for hours listening to music or writing in my journal.

With my mother never coming back for me I felt abandonment which overrode whatever gratitude I wanted to feel. I know now that my mother loved me dearly and only did what she thought was best for me at the time but as a child I could not understand that.

I decided to have Gratitude in my life because I know that it would not only help in my personal growth but it would help in my healing process

The benefits of having Gratitude;

-to feel better instantly

-to enjoy supportive, synergistic, exciting relationships

-to increase prosperity and abundance

-to experience vibrant health

-to have peace of mind

-to supercharge creativity

-to magnetize the realization of my dreams and goals

-to make a profound difference in the lives of many people

As I opened my eyes to more things to be grateful for I realized that I am walking in amazing days. When I opened my eyes I saw the sun shining and felt the breeze blowing. I saw the huge puffy white clouds that were drifting in the sky and as I looked around I knew that I had so much to be grateful for. I am blessed and the Lord always comes through for me even when I least expect it. Things just always seem to have a way of working themselves out in my favor. I inhaled and exhaled a deep breath and realized how grateful I am to have a healthy pair of lungs.

At that moment on the first day of Summer I felt the presence of the Lord surrounding me and I am amazed of all the birds that were singing.

The moment that I focus on how grateful I am, I instantly feel better. I feel good to be alive and take in all of life's grandeur. I have abundance in my life now. At this moment which is the only moment I can live in I have everything I need. I am grateful for my life lessons and I'm at peace with all of my decisions because they have brought me to the moment I am in right now. I cannot live in the past nor in the future only in the moment. Having an attitude of gratitude is very encouraging to me. I feel as if I can take on any challenge that comes my way for it will make me a better person. I realize how blessed I am. I realize how far along I am to be able to meditate on my now and rejoice in all that life has to offer me. I am assured that peace comes from within and not the worldly things that are outward.

Ebony Simms

Gratitude is a gift of Love.

I acknowledge God's love in all things...

Affirmations

-I believe that there is one intelligent substance, from which all things proceed

- I believe that this substance gives me everything I desire

- I relate myself to it by a feeling of deep profound gratitude

My soul will always be grateful so that I can live closer to God. The mental attitude of gratitude draws the mind closer to God. When I fix my mind on the Supreme when good things come to me more good things I will receive. Gratitude will lead my mind to harmony with creative thought and prevent me from falling into competitive thought. Gratitude keeps me from looking at supplies as limited.

Jesus said, "I thanks thee, that thou hearest me." (KJV)

It is gratitude that keeps me connected with power. Without gratitude I cannot keep from having dissatisfied thoughts coming into my mind. The moment I permit my mind to dwell with dissatisfaction I will lose ground and my mind will start to take the form of these things. If I permit my mind to dwell upon inferior it will become inferior. On the other hand if I fix my attention on the best my character will take form of the best and I will receive the best. A grateful mind will continually expect great things. The reaction of gratitude produces faith. I will cultivate a habit of being grateful for every good thing that comes to me and to give thanks continuously. I include all things in my gratitude. I will not waste my time thinking or talking about short comings or wrong actions. Being grateful in all things will bring me into harmonious relations with the good in everything and the good in everything will move towards me.

Ebony Simms

𝔊ratitude takes three forms

-a feeling in the heart

-an expression in words

-a giving in return

𝔍𝔫𝔴𝔞𝔯𝔡 𝔡𝔢𝔳𝔬𝔱𝔦𝔬𝔫 𝔟𝔯𝔦𝔫𝔤𝔰 𝔣𝔬𝔯𝔱𝔥 𝔤𝔯𝔞𝔱𝔦𝔱𝔲𝔡𝔢...

Affirmations

"Today in this moment I am grateful for my peace."

"I am grateful for the love that surrounds me."

"I am grateful for the abundance that I feel in my heart."

I give all praise to God for this feeling of love and peace. I realize that when I turn from Him I feel empty but when I turn towards Him I feel full. God is my refuge and strength a very present help in trouble. God shield me from all harm that comes towards me. My decisions have made me who I am and Gods grace encourages me to keep moving ahead. I will continually praise God and give Him thanksgiving.

I give thanks for my bills because they are blessings that I have already received. I realize that gratitude is energy of the spiritual realm waiting to be tapped by us. Feelings of gratitude are enhanced by our prayerful, conscious meditation.

Gratitude is the mystery that has been eluded for centuries.

𝔄𝔰𝔨 ℚ𝔲𝔢𝔰𝔱𝔦𝔬𝔫𝔰 𝔬𝔣 𝔊𝔯𝔞𝔱𝔦𝔱𝔲𝔡𝔢

Is my attitude holding me back from having my best life?

_____

_____

_____

What can I learn from this experience?

_____

_____

_____

How can I grow from this experience?

_____

_____

_____

What is the blessing in this experience?

_____

_____

_____

What can I take away from this experience that empowers me?

_____

_____

_____

What is the opportunity for me in this experience?

_____

_____

_____

What possibilities does this experience open up for me?

_____

_____

_____

What is the most loving thing to do in this experience?

_____

_____

_____

What am I grateful for?

_____

_____

_____

LORD I THANK YOU

FOR EVERYTHING YOU HAVE
ALLOWED ME TO ACCOMPLISH
FOR TURNING MY LIFE AROUND
FOR MAKING AND MOLDING
ME TO BE A BETTER PERSON
I LOVE YOU LORD
FOR ALLOWING ME TO BE AT PEACE
YOU HAVE BEEN SO GOOD TO ME
FOR THAT I SAY THANK YOU
FOR ALL THE DOORS THAT YOU ARE
CONTINUING TO OPEN IN MY LIFE
FOR LOVING ME IN SPITE OF
ALL MY INIQUITIES
FOR BEING SO PATIENT WITH ME
FOR BRINGING ME OUT OF DARKNESS
FOR RESTORING MY SOUL
FOR LOVING ME SO MUCH
FOR BEING MY FATHER
FOR HOLDING MY HAND
FOR TELLING ME THAT I CAN,
WHEN I HAD DOUBTS
FOR PLACING JOY IN MY LIFE
FOR ALL THESE THINGS AND MANY MORE

Chapter 2

~ Memories/Past ~

I remember being drunk on my eighth birthday but I don't remember if that was the first time I had taken a drink or not. This was the last birthday party I've ever had. I was still living with my mother at this time and there was alcohol all over our apartment. Beer was my drink of choice on this night. I don't remember the name of it but I know it was in a can because I stuck my tongue down in the whole and almost got it stuck in there. My mother was tipsy and found my drinking to be humorous.

Thus, I have also struggled for years with addictions and this one just seemed to linger on. Thinking back I recall my mother, grandmother, great grandmother, aunts, uncles, cousins and biological grandfather all struggling with the addiction of alcohol as well. This for me has been a generational curse and as hard as I have been trying to break the generational curses of my family I realize that I cannot do it alone.

When my brother passed away I was fourteen years old and one of the clearest memories of this day was walking down to the liquor store drive thru and buying a six pack of beer. Before I knew it I drank the entire pack of beer and I realize now that this was my way of numbing the pain that I was dealing with at that time. As the years passed and more pain entered my life I continued to drink heavily and act out of order as a result. My friends and family have laughed it off because they say I don't hurt anyone as a result of my actions but I do. The damage that is done to my insides, the fact that I don't address the real problems that I am facing as a result of the drinking, not to mention how lousy I feel after the drinking high has worn off. I have had too many black outs to count. When I finally come around the next day or so my friends tell me of some of the ways I've behaved and I am totally embarrassed then I start having the flash backs. These are impressions left on my brain which cannot be shaken out. As I move forward I continue to be grateful that today I am sober. We can only be sober one day at a time and today I chose to be.

Ebony Simms

Picture of me at my eight year birthday
party with my mother and brother, had
too much too many beers this night.

I attempted on several occasions to go to AA but learned that I had to surrender myself to God in order to get the real help that I needed. After several failed relationships and finally losing everything I continued to turn to the alcohol. I would be at work and thinking the entire time about the liquor I had stashed at home that I so desperately wanted to get home to.

As mentioned before I had several blackouts from abusing alcohol. On one particular day I went to a pool party where I was mixing drinks white liquor and dark. I didn't feel intoxicated at the party but when I left the party I was real hungry. So after taking my friends home I stopped by the store and purchased some corn chips and chocolate covered raisins. I didn't eat these things I inhaled them I could feel the junk sitting in my chest so I went home and laid in my bed.

I tossed and turned for hours before finally falling off to sleep. My body began to feel horrible I was awaken from my sleep with the urge to vomit and that is what I did for what seemed like the next 24 hours. If it wasn't coming from one end it was coming from the other end without my control. At several times during what I would call alcohol poising I wanted to check myself into the closest hospital but was afraid that I may be recognized. During this entire process I kept receiving calls from a girlfriend asking me about a night club she wanted to attend that night with me. I could not believe I continued to get these calls from her even after I kept telling her I was in no condition to leave out of my house.

While in bed I heard clearly from the Lord saying **"if you continue to live your life in this manner you will surely die young as the rest of your family."** I prayed to God that He give me one more chance and I promised Him that I would do better with my life. For the next week my urine was orange and when I looked this up online, I found that I could be having problems with my liver. From that incident on I have not taken another drink of alcohol!

Some things we have to let go and let God...

I have the courage to move forward.

I leave behind ordinary and walk into extraordinary.

Chapter 3

~ Faith ~

"What do you do when you tried and failed and want to quit?" TD Jakes asks.

You do it again! You have to bounce back and have tenacity. God is going to give you another opportunity, another chance. God said I am going to give you something new to replace something old. Do it again! Even though you may be in a deficit, don't give up. God will restore back the chance that you have lost. God said I will bless you again. I will heal you again. I will give you joy again. I will restore your soul again. God is not finished with you yet.

Broke, lonely, confused, burdened but I'm going to stand any way. Don't throw in the towel bounce back. Fight back! God said you will not die empty. Believe God for a comeback and it will happen. You have to have a relationship with the Lord. I am so grateful that my grandmother introduced me to the Lord when I was real young. Even though I've strayed away I always felt His presence surrounding me and it draws me back in.

Please do not be discouraged. Know that people will try to discourage you for the leap in faith that you are taking. What you are attempting to do has been done by others and it can be done by you! Put God first and the rest will follow. Know that he has not brought you this far to leave you. You must do this by faith and not by sight. Put all of you into it.

If you can put eight hours of work in for someone else you can at least put one hour of work in daily for yourself and your own business. Within six months you will see how far you have come and know that this is God. He told you that you with Him will receive the desires of your heart, as long as you put work in for it.

It's not over get up brush yourself off and don't lose sight of your dreams. No matter all you've been through or who counted you dead it's not over until God says it's over. You are so blessed and your family needs you.

One Sunday morning on my way to do laundry, I drove past a church in Fort Lauderdale, FL. New Mount Olive Baptist Church is on a side street I would not normally take and I saw some really well dressed people going in. I thought to myself I should visit. I would like to know what's going on in there. Later that day a dear friend told me that he thought I should go to this church. All I could do was laugh because I said I just drove past there this morning and was thinking the same thing. A couple of weeks later I looked online to find out the church times and I got dressed to go to the 11 o'clock service.

Listening to the choir and the word of God coming from the Senior Pastor Dr. Marcus D. Davidson I received a touch from God. I knew then I wanted more. When I got there I sat in the back seat next to the door just in case I wanted to make a mad dash! The hand of the Lord touched me in that service and my life has not been the same. I have been hungry for more. What I began to do is after the Sunday services I would go home and do my own Bible study and research. I started with the scriptures that the pastor preached then I began to watch sermons online and read other scriptures.

On my third Sunday there before the pastor could get out that "the doors of the church were open," I hurried to the front to rededicate my life to Christ. As I stood at the alter I accepted Jesus as my personal Savior and I will be forever grateful for the love and compassion I received from First Lady Yvokia Davidson in that moment. By accepting

Jesus Christ as your Lord and Savior he provides a relationship with the Father and eternal life through his death on the cross and resurrection (Rom. 5:10).

Romans 10:9 promises, "If you confess with your mouth Jesus as Lord, and believe in your heart that God raised Him from the dead, you will be saved."

I repeated the words...

Lord Jesus, I ask You to forgive my sins and save me from eternal separation from God. By faith, I accept Your work and death on the cross as sufficient payment for my sins. Thank You for providing the way for me to know You and to have a relationship with my heavenly Father. Through faith in You, I have eternal life. Thank You also for hearing my prayers and loving me unconditionally. Please give me the strength, wisdom, and determination to walk in the center of Your will. In Jesus' name, amen.

I started out just trying to be more grateful and I found Jesus!!!

Two months later I was baptized...

I was baptized on Father's Day

I must have unwavering faith and be able to hold the vision of what I want in my life and this impression is given to the formless, and the creative forces are set in motion.

55 times in Psalms alone we are taught to give thanks to God.

Psalms 86:12

I will give thanks to thee O Lord my God, with all my heart, and will glorify thy name forever.

Gratitude influences all other emotions and virtues.

It is gratitude, which the Lord invokes through the Gospel of His Son.

Matthew 13:12

For whoever has, to him more shall be given, and he will have an abundance; but whoever does not have, even what he has shall be taken away from him.

Or

Whoever has gratitude will be given more, and he or she will have abundance. Whoever does not have gratitude even what he or she has will be taken from him or her.

If you don't take the time to be grateful you will never have more, and what you do have you will lose.

"Like attracts like"

𝔖ome things to ponder

Gratitude protects against legalism.
Thankfulness to God will overflow
as a testimony of Him.
Gratitude causes the outpouring
of praise to Him.
Thankfulness to God is an indication
of spiritual maturity.
Being truly thankful is God's will for us.
Thankfulness should characterize
our personality.
Gratitude is an essential part
of a healthy prayer life.
Gratitude is faith in action and it
connects us to the supply source.
It is easy to get stuck in self-pity but
gratitude acts with the precision of the
scalpel of the surgeon in getting beneath
such energy draining states and leveraging
up a wonderful inspiration from within.
Gratitude is a hallmark of humanity; it lifts
our lives out of ignorance and isolation.
Gratitude is a choice!

Chapter 4

~ 𝔉𝔞𝔪𝔦𝔩𝔶 ~

I am grateful for getting a glimpse of sun on my skin with its warm rays and the cool breeze. As I sit and reflect on my life I'm so grateful for my family. I love them with all my heart. I'm ever so grateful for the ones that are still alive and even the ones that have passed on. For the ones that have passed on I hold on to the dearest memories of them and I cherish those forever.

When I think of my family I include my close dear friends to this list. There are friends that I have known since grade school and friends that I have met along my journey. I have learned in life that not everyone stays with you on your journey they come for seasons and reasons and for that I've learned to be grateful. Instead of saying the friendship or the family relationship is over I just say, "I have gone as far as I'm going to go with you on your journey."

I am on a wonderful journey called Life.

With the loss of so many dear love ones that were close to me, I had to finally make peace with their passing. I had to begin to take their life experiences and grow from them. I had to begin to take pieces from their life to keep my own life encouraged. I was often panged (having deep emotional distress) reflecting back on how my mother, brother, grandmother, aunt and grandfather all died. That was a great deal of hurt for me. Then I had to look at how selfish I was being while considering that nothing was left behind by them that they could pass on or leave to me as far as possessions. Moving forward in my personal growth I came to realize that their legacy, personal characteristics, traditions, and beliefs these are the real tangible things that I could cherish!

From my mother I learned not to give up. I learned from her not to throw in the towel on life. By watching my mother's life deteriorate before my very eyes I learned strength. My mother taught me kindness she was woman with a huge heart. My brother taught me charm and charisma. He had a smile that would make your heart feel like it was going to jump out of your chest. He was also my protector I have often felt his presence surrounding me when I faced some of my life challenges. My grandmother taught me love and compassion. This woman gave when she had nothing left to even give herself. She taught me to toughen up, to shake loose of the things that life holds over you. My aunt, I laugh and can't hide a smile when she comes to mind. From her I can still hear the valuable lessons on life and men. She would tell me, "You do alright and then you get low." To me this meant that you will start off on a good tract but somewhere along the way you get lost. The key was to find your way back. She would also say, "You're going to pay getting on the bus, or you are going to pay getting off, either way you are going to pay." To me this meant you cannot out slick life. If you do wrong it will catch up to you. My grandfather taught me that a man is supposed to provide for his family.

There were also some very negative things I learned from all of these loved ones. What I chose to take from the negative was how to move away from those things in my life before I get to the second half of my life. I have decided that I am going to be my own experiment in changing my life for the better by developing gratitude habits. Developing these gratitude habits have ultimately allowed me to make the great shift in my life.

After dealing with the loss in my life I rejoice in the now and the future. I am so grateful for my daughters for they continue to teach me patience, tenderness and respect for myself. When I think of them I hold myself to a higher standard. I want to be a greater example of what a mother should be even if our arrangement is unconventional. I love them with all of my heart and enjoy growing and learning life lessons with them.

One of the quotes I gave to a few members in my family that were feeling down on their luck.

"Day by day, in every way, I'm getting better and better." Emile Coue

I have watched how it has changed their lives. For as often as I think of this quote throughout the day (when I recite it) I begin to feel better.

Each and every day you have to work on personal development. It takes work to become a better person...

"Expressing gratitude for what we already have enables it to grow." Louise L. Hay

Like the Law of Gravity, the power of Gratitude works without us even knowing how or why.

Chapter 5

~ Health/Fasting/Prayer ~

I am grateful for my breath, the oxygen that fills my lungs.

As I began to walk more closely with the Holy Spirit I wanted to put things in my body that would allow me to have a healthy lifestyle. I stopped drinking alcohol and taking drugs. I also began to stop eating animal products. To each its own on what you put into your body but for me this has helped me to live a better life.

Around the time I rededicated my life to Christ I took a pledge to practice abstinence from sex and alcohol. I didn't need any static in my life or anything to come in between and my relationship with God. As I was reaching my first 30 days of abstinence I went on a 3 days fasting/prayer. During this time I looked up everything I could find on the subject and came to Isaiah 58:3-12

³ 'Why have we fasted,' they say,

    'and you have not seen it?
Why have we humbled ourselves,
    and you have not noticed?'
"Yet on the day of your fasting, you do as you please
    and exploit all your workers.

⁴ Your fasting ends in quarreling and strife,
    and in striking each other with wicked fists.
You cannot fast as you do today
    and expect your voice to be heard on high.
⁵ Is this the kind of fast I have chosen,
    only a day for people to humble themselves?
Is it only for bowing one's head like a reed
    and for lying in sackcloth and ashes?
Is that what you call a fast,
    a day acceptable to the LORD?

⁶ "Is not this the kind of fasting I have chosen:
to loose the chains of injustice
    and untie the cords of the yoke,
to set the oppressed free
    and break every yoke?
⁷ Is it not to share your food with the hungry
    and to provide the poor wanderer with shelter—
when you see the naked, to clothe them,
    and not to turn away from your own flesh and
    blood?
⁸ Then your light will break forth like the dawn,

and your healing will quickly appear;
then your righteousness will go before you,
> and the glory of the LORD will be your rear
> guard.
9 Then you will call, and the LORD will answer;
> you will cry for help, and he will say: Here am I.

"If you do away with the yoke of oppression,
> with the pointing finger and malicious talk,
10 and if you spend yourselves in behalf of the
hungry
> and satisfy the needs of the oppressed,
then your light will rise in the darkness,
> and your night will become like the noonday.
11 The LORD WILL GUIDE YOU ALWAYS;
> he will satisfy your needs in a sun-scorched
> land
> and will strengthen your frame.
You will be like a well-watered garden,
> like a spring whose waters never fail.
12 Your people will rebuild the ancient ruins
> and will raise up the age-old foundations;
you will be called Repairer of Broken Walls,
> Restorer of Streets with Dwellings.

I wanted to put away this sin once and for all.

The Bible says when you fast not if you fast...my flesh is weak but my spirit grew strong! When I came off my fast I went to my first AA meeting and saw before my eyes what my life could have turned out to be if I didn't draw myself closer to God. I am so in love with Him now and constantly ask for forgiveness for turning away from Him so long. When I got home from my first AA meeting I turned on my Gospel music and gave Him praise I thanked Him for always having a hedge of protection around me. I could actually see the hedge in my minds eye that every time I strayed I could only go but so far before I would be brought back. I will ever be grateful for Divine Providence!

There are many forms of fasting. You have to be led by God as to which fast is right for you. Now I alternate between a 24 hour fast, the day of my choosing or I skip one meal at any part of the day.

Life is something to be grateful for.

When we change the way we think and start to fill our lives with thankfulness nothing else is the same. We start to change our lives forever and it does get better.

Being grateful for bad things that happen is not about laying down like a doormat; ready for the next punch life might throw at us. It's more about learning to live with the life you've had and seeing the good that can spring from anything.

I have to see my struggle, hurt, abuse and injuries as how I rose above it all and keep on going. The key is not to see my situation as something that broke me but something that made me.

I am grateful for still being alive, still surviving, still fighting and learning from the lessons life has thrown my way either at my hands or the hands of others.

The turning point in my life came when I began to realize that I can walk away from an abusive relationship. I have allowed a lot of that behavior to happen around me and I've learned from it.

I look at life differently now and I am grateful to be able to stand up for myself.

Everyday six feet above ground is a gift.

Nietzsche said, "What doesn't kill us only makes us stronger."

It works if you choose the path of love and forgiveness.

Forgiveness is about what happens to your own heart during the process.

The law operates on your thoughts and feelings because they are energy too, so whatever you think, whatever you feel, you attract to you.

So if you are finding things to be grateful for you will attract more things to you to be grateful for.

Instead of focusing on what could have been.

-which leads to a stronger sense of loss and hurt

-which is very difficult to move on from

I chose to focus on how it's shaped me, and given me a different perspective then I can take on a more positive role.

You must work on your self-image...

Your self-image can be changed!

Once the concept of self is changed other things consistent with the new concept of self are accomplished easily and without strain.

If my imagination is vivid enough and detailed enough of the way I want to see myself this practice is equivalent to an actual experience as far as the nervous system is concerned.

We have to be careful of how we describe ourselves. We constantly walk around talking about I am sick, I am broke, I am this or I am that...Instead we must begin to change our self-talk.

I am in God...
God is in me...
I Am That, I Am
Become conscious of how I use I Am...
I am strong
I am perfect
I am successful
I am love
I am able
I am prosperous
I am grateful
I am healthy
I am sober
I am rich
I am wealthy
I am patience
I am peace
I am a bestselling author...;)
I am a mother
I am a friend
I am strong
I am at my ideal body weight

If it doesn't feel natural it isn't going to work.

We spend a big portion of our time worrying about things that never even happen. I am grateful for seeing another day.

A noble person is mindful and thankful of the favors he receives from others –The Budda

Chapter 6

~ Financial/Give to Receive ~

Gratitude is the key element in the attainment of happiness, wealth, relationship harmony and overall success.

Be grateful before you even receive anything.

Gratitude is an attitude that can usher abundance in our life very quickly if you apply yourself diligently.

Gratitude may be the fastest single pathway to happiness, health, long life and prosperity.

Gratitude is magnetic and the more gratitude you have the more abundance you magnetize. It is Universal law!

Every action always has an opposite and equal reaction. Newton

As I began to give my offerings to the church that I decided was my home, my life instantly changed... every two or three days I would check the mail and there would appear checks in my mailbox!!!

This was totally forgotten about money that I had no idea would ever come my way!

My heart began to cry out to God...the more I showed gratitude and thanked Him another unexpected check would appear in the mail!!!!

As I write these words my eyes tear up because on my vision board I wrote out a check to myself for $1,000,000.00 and I believe with all my heart that it's on the way and I am open to receiving it!!!

When you arise in the morning, give thanks for the morning light, for your life and strength. Give thanks for your food and joy of living. If you see no reason for giving thanks, the fault lies with yourself. Tecumseh (1768-1813) Shawnee Native American Leader

You have to practice gratitude so that it becomes a habit.

Gratitude changed me, my whole life magically changed.

Gratitude works like magic.

Gratitude is a feeling.

The more sincerely grateful you are the faster your life will change.

I came home after my meditation on the beach and was surprised to see an unexpected check in the mail from my publishing company. I am so grateful because it was money I didn't have. I thank God for every check that I receive. God is blessing me right now!

Ebony Simms

Think about what you are grateful for...

I love my job

My family is very supportive

I had the best vacation ever

I feel amazing today

I received the biggest tax refund ever

I had a great weekend

Chapter 7

~ 𝔘𝔫𝔦𝔳𝔢𝔯𝔰𝔞𝔩 𝔏𝔬𝔳𝔢 ~

Galatians 5:13–15 the good news of Christ is a call to freedom. God's revealed will for all of us is that we have the opportunity, the ability, and the desire to do what will give us the greatest satisfaction now and in a thousand years. The only activity which we can perform in freedom is love. "You were called to freedom . . . so through love be servants of one another" (Galatians 5:13). This love is not optional. It is commanded. And it is very radical: "You shall love your neighbor as yourself." In other words, we are called in our freedom to desire and seek the happiness of others with the same zeal that we seek our own.

Paul's answer to this discouragement is found in Galatians 5:16–18. The secret is in learning to "walk by the Spirit" (Galatians 5:16). If the Christian life looks too hard, we must remember that we are not called to live it by ourselves. We must live it by the Spirit of God. The command of love is not a new legalistic burden laid on our back; it is what happens freely when we walk by the Spirit. People who try to love without relying on God's Spirit always wind up trying to fill their own emptiness rather than sharing their fullness. And so love ceases to be love. Love is not easy for us. But the good news is that it is not primarily our work but God's. We must simply learn to "walk by the Spirit."

<u>Love</u> needs to be based in <u>gratitude;</u> and <u>gratitude</u> needs to be based in <u>love</u>.

These two words together create the most important vibration.

When we practice an attitude of gratitude we are practicing feeling loved.

Grace is our response to feeling love unconditionally by God.

> In all things I am grateful my heart is open and ready to receive love. My ears are open and ready to receive instructions. My eyes are open and ready to receive vision. My mind is open and ready to receive knowledge and wisdom. My mouth is open and ready to be fed the fruit of the spirit. I am connected to the Source. I am in God and He in is me.

Lord I ask that you teach me how to love. Show me how to love. I am learning how to deal with my emotions.

I feel the love of the Universe.

All is love. Love is waiting to be expressed. When I think I don't have love I just look inside. I have a deep love inside me. Until I love myself I cannot express love to anyone else. I love myself no one is going to treat me better than I treat myself.

If I haven't been doing this now is the time.

Gratitude A, B, C's

Attitude of Gratitude
Believe
Conquer
Deliverance
Excellence
Fantastic
Grateful
Happy
Incredible
Joyous
Kindness
Laughter
Money
Nostalgia
Optimism
Prayer
Quintessential
Respect
Spectacular
Treasures
Ultimate
Vivacious
Willing
Xtraordinary
Yes I Can!
Zealous

I suggest you make your own list

5 Ways to Cultivate Gratitude In your life

Keep a journal

-The pen is mightier than a sword as I connect to a state of appreciation as I record my expressions of gratitude. Daily I have been reflecting so that I could put pen to paper and capture the moments that are meaningful to my life.

Write letters of appreciation

-The ball is in my court and I have to do something before any progress can be made in a situation. How can you express your love and heartfelt feelings towards another?

Make gratitude visits

-I hold the cards now it's time to be selective. Go visit people that will put you in a mindset of gratitude.

Make gratitude lists

-Introspection...I have control over my emotional set points and I can set them to feel good. List the things you are grateful for.

Take gratitude walks

Ebony Simms

-Play some music that makes you feel good and go on a brisk walk. Get some vitamin D in your system. Take long deep breaths and begin to feel good!

Dear Negative,

To all the negative things that I have brought into my life I would like to say thank you immensely for allowing me to grow into the woman I am today. You have taught me that whatever does not kill me only makes me stronger.

Oh negative thinking, oh negative acting, oh negative days, years, decades I wish you all the best and send you my regards for the day has come where the rain is gone and the sun is shining ever so bright.

Sincerely,

Ebony Simms

𝕰𝖛𝖊𝖗𝖞𝖉𝖆𝖞 𝖑𝖎𝖛𝖎𝖓𝖌 𝖗𝖊𝖖𝖚𝖎𝖗𝖊𝖘 𝖈𝖔𝖚𝖗𝖆𝖌𝖊...

My thoughts are in training. The sun is shining ever so brightly. I love the life that I am in. I am grateful to finally have some peace. God has shown me great things and I know that if I am grateful in the small things I will have an abundance to come. I can finally say that I feel love unconditionally. I am love, I radiate love and I receive it now. I receive love now. I have money in the bank and a place to comfortably lay my head at night. I have freedom to move about. I love it. I was not in this grateful place before but now that I am I embrace it. I hold on to it and I allow it into my life now and forever more.

Most people don't know how brave they really are. Our thoughts effect what is coming. Our mental intentions, or stretching our thoughts outward actually link us to objects and draw them towards us.

I am grateful in this moment.

I'm sitting in the shade and enjoying the cool breeze against my skin. I am enjoying life and happy to be a part of it. God's grace has carried me so far and continues to carry me every day of my life.

A friend said to me jokingly that I am in control and he was right...I am in control and I believe that the Universe is giving me a do over. A second chance at life one where I am in control to create my own destiny and this time I choose to be grateful in all things.

I love myself. I thank God for hearing me when I called.

Since I've been doing my gratitude research I've been in a better mood.

The world is changing and my world especially. I am processing better thoughts.

I feel in great spirits because I've chosen to decide how I'm going to process life issues.

Be a catalyst for change.

Reconnect to the divine. Believe in a Higher Power!

Everything you can see, touch or feel is something to be in gratitude for.

Gratitude opens the door to abundance.

When you change yourself you change the world.

Gratitude can take us from feeling sorry for ourselves to feeling joy.

Restructure your brain to develop social intelligence.

Let go of Limiting beliefs.

Gratitude saved my life.

I am grateful for my life.

My mood, thoughts and attitude changed as I practiced gratitude.

What are you grateful for today?

When you practice gratitude you change yourself and when you change yourself you change the world.

A song that touches my soul every time I hear it is by Bishop Hezekiah Xzavier Walker, Jr. *'Grateful'*

When Gratitude took over my life I began to only listen to inspirational music because anything else would not sit well with my spirit.

3 things to get your gratitude in motion

You have to feel the emotions of gratitude.

_____

_____

_____

You have to express your gratitude to others.

_____

_____

_____

You have to do daily gratitude exercises.

_____

_____

_____

Last night I fell off into a deep sleep then I woke up around 3am and could not fall back to sleep. I began to replay in my mind all the things I am grateful for. I don't remember if it was the first sleep I went into or the second but I kept repeating 'Thank you' over and over again. I then thought of the things that I was grateful for over and over. Not only did I say thank you but I attached a thankful heart to it as well. From that all I could feel is love.

.

Writing, researching and putting what I have researched into words that I understand is a passion of mine. I enjoy writing and hours can pass as I do so. I am on a quest for purpose in my life and how can I use this purpose to help others.

I want to know Gods thoughts. Albert Einstein

I am grateful today for all the things that are showing up in my life to remind me of how grateful I truly am. I am grateful for being able to help my friends when they are in need. I am also grateful for being able to call my friends and tell them when I am in need of their prayers and encouragement.

GRATITUDE

Grow
Remember
Accept
Trade
Invoke
Treasure
Understand
Delight
Explore

Gratitude has blossomed me like a flower...

As below, so above; and as above so below,
with this knowledge alone you may work miracles.
The Emerald Tablet

Ebony Simms

When you change!

I had to decide that if I didn't make this change I would die! That is how traumatic it was for me. I would often say this is a life or death situation for me when people would ask why I made such a sudden change in my life.

They may not be aware of it but their intention is to keep you in the trap. Having a herd mentality and herd behavior have been prevalent descriptors for human behavior since people began to form tribes, migrate in groups, and perform cooperative marketing and agricultural functions. The idea of a "group mind" or "mob behavior" was first put forward by 19th-century French social psychologists Gabriel Tarde and Gustave Le Bon.

The herd mentality is like crabs in a barrel. They want you to stay with them but you can't. You have to be the one to elevate your mind no matter what they say or how they make you feel about the changes you are making in your life. You have to encourage yourself and find others that you can connect with that will also encourage you in your new walk of life. Keep in mind the inability or refusal to listen to one's own instinct or 'gut feeling' but to instead follow the majority for fear of being wrong, ostracized or ridiculed is being in a herd. If a herd of animals were headed for a cliff, for the sake of a herd mentality, I doubt one would veer off or stop to save its own life and you have actually taken the steps to change your own life!

Since I made my change I have had the closest people around me doubt me, ridicule me, mock me, have sarcasm towards me, be scornful towards me, sneer at me, belittle me, humiliate me, leer at me, taunt me, tease me and even lie on me. I remember when I stopped hanging out in night clubs and being more selective about where I would go out and the company I would keep a girlfriend of mine would tell me that now I'm acting like an old lady. When I made any attempts on telling her how she should change her life she would tear me apart and list what I used to do or how I used to behave.

They have done all these things because they wanted me to stay in the trap with them. You have to know that you will make people around you look bad because you become their mirror. They often feel they are being exposed. They will warn you about your new way of life and how it's not easy to live this type of lifestyle. They will even tell you about others that have tried and miserably failed. When I began to make my change my friends were nervous for me they were so afraid of what my fall back would be once I give up on my new way thinking. They often feared more for me than I feared for myself.

I had to realize that for things to get better for me I would have to change them. If I wanted things to change I would have to change them for myself. There will be some people for your change and some against your change but you will have to do what is best for you.

The Universe is within me and it's my choice to have an Attitude of Gratitude...

Lost 60 pounds on a low carb diet
with moderate exercise